ZERO TO TEN

For Matteo, SS
For Vanessa and Mark, SN

This edition published in 2003

Publisher: Anna McQuinn
Art Director: Tim Foster
Publishing Assistant: Vikram Parashar

First published in Great Britain in 2003 by Zero To Ten Limited
327 High Street, Slough, Berkshire, SL1 1TX

Copyright © 2003 Zero to Ten Limited
Text copyright © 2003 Simona Sideri
Illustrations copyright © 2003 Sheilagh Noble

A CIP catalogue record for this book is available from
the British Library.

ISBN 1-84089-275-7

Printed in Hong Kong

# Let's look at
# EYES

Written by
**Simona Sideri**

Illustrated by
**Sheilagh Noble**

Look at me, I use my eyes to see!

Eagles have excellent eyes!
They can spot their prey
from high in the sky.

Camels have bushy brows
that shade their eyes
from the burning, desert sun.

They also have long eyelashes
to protect them from flying sand

Owls don't move their eyes, so they always look as if they're staring.

Instead, they turn their
heads right around
        to see in
            all directions!

Bushbabies can see in the dark.

They are nifty night hunters.

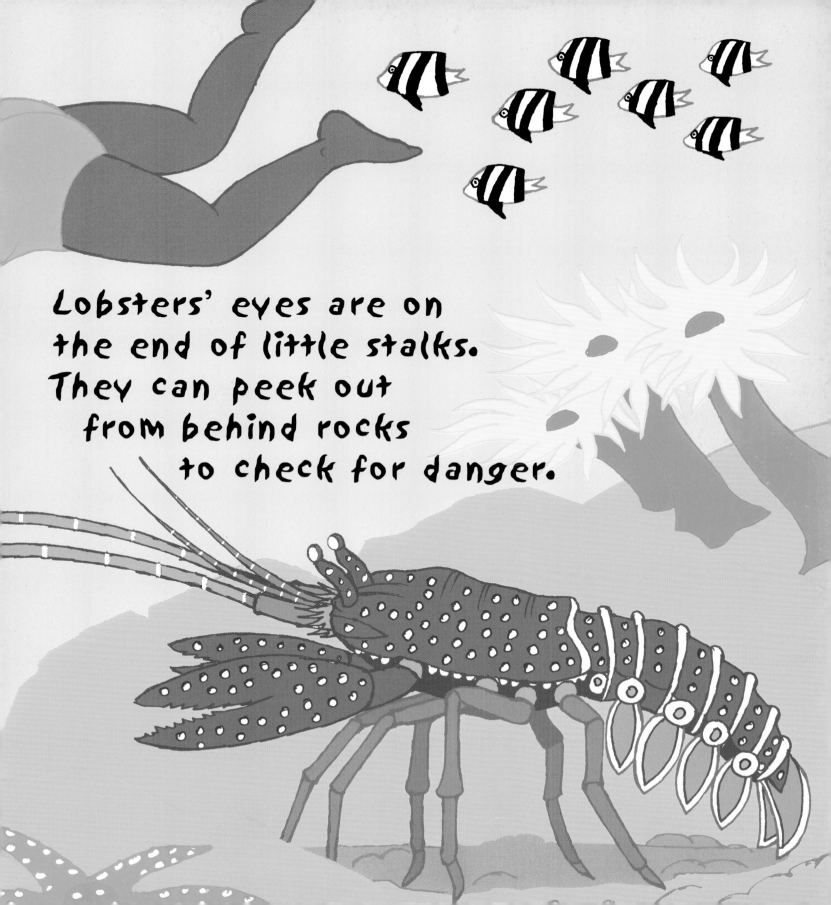

Lobsters' eyes are on
the end of little stalks.
They can peek out
   from behind rocks
      to check for danger.

Wasps have amazing eyes,
made up of many parts.

Each part of the eye
sees just a small part
of whatever they are looking at!

# Eyes are excellent!

 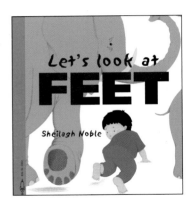 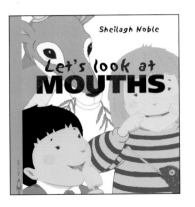 

Hardback
ISBN 1-84089-145-9

Paperback
ISBN 1-84089-273-0

Hardback
ISBN 1-84089-144-0

Paperback
ISBN 1-84089-274-9

Hardback
ISBN 1-84089-147-5

Paperback
ISBN 1-84089-276-5

Hardback
ISBN 1-84089-146-7

Paperback
ISBN 1-84089-275-7

## "SEARCH FOR THE ROCKET"

ZERO TO TEN publishes quality picture books for children aged between zero and ten and we have lots more great books about animals!
Our books are available from all good bookstores.

If you have any problems obtaining any title, or would like to receive information about our books, please contact the publishers:
ZERO TO TEN  327 High Street, Slough, Berkshire SL1 1TX  Tel: 01753 578 499  Fax: 01753 578 488